Microwave Mug Meals Made Easy

Sweet and Savory Microwave Meals Cookbook for One

Copyright © 2022 Lion Weber Publishing

ISBN: 978-3-949717-20-8

THANK YOU FOR YOUR PURCHASE!

DO YOU LIKE LION WEBER PUBLISHING?

SUBSCRIBE TO OUR NEWSLETTER AND

DOWNLOAD YOUR FREE GIFT NOW!

DISCOVER THE SECRETS TO THE FOUNTAIN YOUTH

AND TOP HABIT HACKS WITH THESE

8 POWERFUL VIDEO COURSE!

https:// l.ead.me/lwp-free-gift

Table of Contents

Tips to Consider While Cooking
in the Microwave

1. Microwave wattages can differ. The strength of individual microwaves can vary, so the first time you make them, you'll need to experiment a bit to make sure that the cooking time is the perfect length of baking time.

    My microwave is 1100 watts. If your wattage is higher or lower, you may need to adjust the cooking time.

    If you don't know what the wattage of your oven is, then there is a water test that you can undertake. For this, place a microwave-safe measuring glass filled with water. Heat the cup on high heat until the water boils.

    If it takes less than three minutes for the water to boil, your oven is about 600 to 700 watts. In contrast, if the microwave takes more than three or four minutes, your oven is 500 to 600 watts. And if it takes more than four minutes to boil the water in the cup, the oven has a power of fewer than 500 watts.

    Some of the common ones are:

    ➢   600-800w – Lower Wattage Microwaves: More time is often needed

    ➢   900-1100w – Average Wattage Microwaves

    ➢   1200-1300w – High Wattage Microwaves: Less time often needed

    If you have a lower-wattage microwave, you will likely need to cook the fare a little longer. On the other hand, if your microwave is stronger than 1000 watts, you will need to reduce cooking time or cooking power.

2. I recommend using a 12 oz. or 15-oz mug typically. To determine how many ounces your mug holds, fill it to the top with water. Then pour the water into a liquid measuring cup. The best container to use in microwaves are mugs, ceramic mugs, ceramic ramekins, glasses, and jars.

    Always use a large mug so no overflow will mess up your microwave. The mug should only be half full prior or a maximum of three-fourths before baking. Avoid using tall & skinny mugs since it will be difficult for the meals to cook evenly.

3. Desserts especially can dry out fast in the microwave. Therefore, cook for the minimum required time and then cook more if needed.

4. When using self-rising flour, ensure that it is not old. Since only a few ingredients are used while making mug cakes, use quality ingredients as it will significantly determine the final product's taste. The baking powder in it may no longer be effective, preventing your mug cake from rising properly.

5. When stirring, ensure that nothing is stuck to the bottom of the mug. Moreover, use a fork instead of a spoon since it helps better in breaking apart the lumps.

6. To check whether the mug cake is cooked, touch the top portion of the cake gently. If it is firm to touch and bounce back, it means it is cooked. If not, cook for 2 to 3 minutes or as required. In contrast, if it doesn't stick, it has been overcooked.

7. Mug cakes will always sink down once it is taken out of the microwave oven.

8. Mug cakes can become spongy if the batter is overmixed and the butter temperature is wrong. Similarly, too much oil and overcooking can also cause it to be rubbery.

9. While cooking, keep a close eye on the mug, so it doesn't overfill or overcook.

BREAKFAST

1. Egg Muffin

This egg muffin made in the microwave is a protein-loaded brekkie that you can make within 5 minutes. On top, it can keep you satiated for a long time!

Preparation Time: 5 Minutes
Cooking Time: 1 Minute
Servings: 1
Ideal Size of the Mug: 14 oz.

Ingredients:

- 2 tbsp. or 20gm Egg
- 5 tbsp. or 40gm All Purpose Flour
- 1 Egg or 40gm, medium
- ¼ tsp. or 1.2gm Baking Powder
- ½ tsp. or 3gm Salt

- 1 tbsp. or 14.7gm Cheddar Cheese, grated
- 1/8 tsp. Baking Soda
- 1 tbsp. or approx. 18gm Onions, finely chopped
- 1 to 2 or 22gm Broccoli Florets
- 2 tsp. or 9.4gm Butter, salted
- 2 tbsp. or 30.4gm Milk

Method of Preparation:

1) To start with, combine flour, salt, baking soda, and powder in a large-sized microwave-safe mug with a spoon or fork.

2) After that, pour milk, 2 tbsp. of egg and melted butter into it, along with onion and cheese.

3) Now, make a well in the center of the mix and spoon in the egg.

4) Then, mix in the batter from the mug's sides over the egg. Stir well.

5) Finally, place the mug in the microwave and cook for 45 seconds or until the top portion is firm to touch. Tip: It might even take up to 1 minute and 15 seconds. Cooking time varies with the microwave wattage.

6) Serve it warm.

Tips:

- Make sure to watch the mug closely while heating to avoid over-cooking and over-flow.

- 1 small egg is around 4 tablespoons, so for 2 tablespoons, consider removing half the portion.

- If desired, add toppings like bacon, sausage, extra cheese, diced veggies, etc., into it.

- Instead of Cheddar cheese, you can use your choice of grated cheese for the recipe.

- Instead of melted butter, you can use vegetable oil.

- To make it keto-friendly, substitute all-purpose flour with almond flour.

Nutritional Information per serving:

- **Calories**: 347Kcal
- **Carbohydrates**: 30.8g
- **Fat**: 18.1g
- **Proteins:** 14.2g

2. Egg Omelette

Light and fluffy, this omelette made in the microwave is so easy to make and is perfect for those busy mornings. Furthermore, they can keep you full for a long time.

Preparation Time: 5 Minutes

Cooking Time: 2 to 3 Minutes

Servings: 1

Ideal Size of the Mug: 12 to 16 oz.

Ingredients:

- 2 Eggs or 80gm, medium
- 1 tbsp. or 15ml Milk
- ¼ of 1 Bell Pepper or 35gm, finely diced
- Kosher Salt, as needed
- 2 Ham Slices, chopped 0r 56gm
- 1 tsp. Chives, finely chopped
- Black Pepper, freshly ground, as needed
- 1 tsp. Sausage Crumbles, cooked (Optional)

Method of Preparation:

1) Combine eggs and milk in a large microwave-safe greased mug with a fork until mixed well. Tip: It is advisable to use a large-sized cup so that it doesn't bubble over quickly since the egg expands while cooking,

2) After that, add all the remaining ingredients and stir well. Tip: Make sure not to overfill it.

3) Heat in the microwave for 30 seconds on high heat. Stir and then cook again for another 30 seconds. Stir and repeat the procedure 2 to 3 times or

until the egg is cooked. Tip: Keep a close watch to ensure the egg doesn't bubble over.

4) Serve it warm.

Tips:

- Grease the mug either with olive oil or spray it with cooking oil spray. Use butter for more flavor.

- This recipe is highly customizable as you can add any of your favorite omelette ingredients to it. Cheese, mushrooms, shredded turkey or chicken, hot sauce, cherry tomatoes, etc., are all excellent choices.

- Based on the number of add-ins, consider increasing the cooking time if needed.

- If you prefer, add a tablespoon of grated cheddar cheese for more flavor.

- Each egg can absorb up to 1 tbsp of liquid. Therefore, we are adding milk which will make it fluffier.

Nutritional Information per serving:

- **Calories**: 196Kcal
- **Carbohydrates**: 2g
- **Fat**: 14g
- **Proteins:** 15g

3. Quiche

A high-protein breakfast quiche with a creamy texture comes your way through this easy recipe.

Preparation Time: 5 Minutes
Cooking Time: 3 Minutes
Servings: 1

Ingredients:

- 1 Egg (40gm), medium
- ½ cup or 15gm Spinach
- 1/3 cup or 81ml of Milk
- 1 tbsp. or 15gm Cream Cheese
- Kosher Salt, as needed
- 1/3 cup or 78.3gm Cheddar Cheese, shredded
- Black Pepper, freshly ground, as needed
- 1 Bacon or 8gm, cooked

Method of Preparation:

1) Begin by cracking an egg into a greased microwave-safe bowl and whisk it with a fork.

2) After that, stir in the spinach to it.

3) Then, add milk and the remaining ingredients to it. Stir well.

4) Place the mug into the microwave and heat on high heat for 3 minutes or until cooked while covering it with a paper towel. Tip: Halfway through the cooking time, check the consistency. If the quiche seems watery, they need more time. On the other hand, if it is slightly puffed up and the eggs are set, it means it is done right.

5) Allow it to cool for a minute or two after it is done.

6) Serve it warm and top it with fresh herbs like parsley and chives if desired.

Tips:

- You can use fresh or frozen spinach. Remove as much water as possible from the spinach if you use a frozen one, as it will otherwise make the quiche watery.

- If desired, add cherry tomatoes for more flavor and nutrition.

- Another excellent choice to consider is bread slices broken into cubes.

- Instead of bacon, you can add ham.

- Instead of cheddar cheese, you can use mozzarella cheese.

- For a richer flavor, substitute milk with half and a half or heavy cream.

Variations:

- If you prefer quiche with crust, add 4 tbsp. of all-purpose flour, a pinch of baking soda, and powder.

Nutritional Information per serving:

- **Calories**: 259Kcal
- **Carbohydrates**: 5.4g
- **Fat**: 18.6g

- **Proteins:** 18g

4. Oatmeal in a Mug

Vegan & gluten-free, this hearty oatmeal made in the microwave is perfect for those hectic mornings when you have no time to waste. On top, it is super-creamy, delicious, and fluffy without being mushy!

Preparation Time: 5 Minutes
Cooking Time: 2 to 3 Minutes
Servings: 1
Ideal Size of the Mug: 16 oz.

Ingredients:

- ¼ tsp. or 0.7gm Cinnamon
- ½ cup or 120ml Milk, whole
- Dash of Salt
- ½ cup or 45gm Old-Fashioned Oats
- 1 tsp. or 4.2gm Vanilla Extract
- Sweetener of your choice, as needed

Method of Preparation:

1) To start with, mix milk, oats, cinnamon, salt, and vanilla in a large & deep microwave mug and combine it well. Tip: The ratio between milk and oats should ideally be 1:1. But if you prefer a looser consistency, you can add more milk.

2) Next, heat the mixture on high heat for 1 minute and 15 seconds or 90 seconds or until it gets a soft and chewable consistency. Set it aside for a minute.

3) Now, sweeten it with your choice of sweetener and stir well. Tip: If it seems too dry, add a bit of milk at the end and cover it with a plate for 1 to 2 minutes to make it fluffier. Or you can microwave it for another 30 seconds after adding milk.

4) Serve it warm.

Tips:

- Grease the mug with cooking oil spray.

- Make sure to use old–fashioned rolled oats and avoid using instant oats.

- You can top it with peanut butter, nuts, chia seeds, dried or fresh berries, honey, banana, etc.

- Instead of cinnamon, you can add nutmeg or ground cloves

- Instead of dairy milk, you can use any nut milk. Water can also be used, but the flavor would be less.

- The chance of exploding happens when the liquid boils too rapidly and doesn't have enough space inside. If it happens, reduce the power and increase the cooking time, so the liquid doesn't boil rapidly. Furthermore, do not cover the mug while cooking.

- If you add ½ tablespoon of cashew butter along with 2 teaspoons of maple syrup and one tablespoon of chocolate chips, you can get cookie dough-style oatmeal.

Variations:

- If you like peanut butter, you can make peanut butter oatmeal by placing it on the bottom of the bowl before adding oats and milk. Stir halfway through so that it gets mixed evenly. And then top it with more peanut butter.

Nutritional Information per serving:

- **Calories**: 240Kcal
- **Carbohydrates**: 34g
- **Fat**: 6g
- **Proteins**: 9g

5. Baked Oatmeal

Nutritious yet easy to make, this tangy blueberry-flavored baked oatmeal is packed with goodness and flavor. Moreover, it is highly customizable since you can add your favorite ingredients to it.

Preparation Time: 5 Minutes
Cooking Time: 2 to 3 Minutes
Servings: 1
Ideal Size of the Mug: 12 to 16 oz.

Ingredients:

- ½ cup or 45gm Old-fashioned Rolled Oats
- 1/3 cup or 55.4gm Blueberries
- 1 tbsp. or 7gm Flax Seeds, ground
- 1/3 cup Banana or 100gm, mashed
- 2 tsp. or 13.2gm Maple Syrup
- ¼ tsp. or 0.7gm Cinnamon
- ½ cup Almond Milk or 120ml, unsweetened

Method of Preparation:

1) Begin by placing all the ingredients needed to make the baked oatmeal, excluding blueberries, in the greased microwave mug.

2) Mix them well and top them with the blueberries.

3) Cook on high heat for 2 to 3 minutes or until cooked. Tip: If you want it with a cookie texture, go for 2 minutes. But then, if you prefer a cake texture, go for 3 minutes.

4) Add nut butter or yogurt if desired.

5) Serve it warm.

Tips:

- Grease the mug either with olive oil or spray it with cooking oil spray. Use butter for more flavor.

- To get 1/3rd cup of mashed banana, you would require approximately more than ½ but less than ¾ of one whole banana.

- If desired, you can grind the oats and use oats flour for making the recipe.

- Instead of blueberries, you can use diced strawberries, apples, peaches, or pears.

- Cinnamon can be substituted with other spices like nutmeg, allspice, pumpkin spice, etc.

- You can add nuts, shredded coconut, or chocolate chips if desired.

Variation:

- For a cakey texture, you can grind all the ingredients in a blender and blend until smooth. Pour the batter into the greased mug and cook on high heat for 1 minute to 1 ½ minute.

Nutritional Information per serving:

- **Calories**: 401Kcal
- **Carbohydrates**: 63.6g
- **Fat**: 11.2g
- **Proteins:** 14.5g

6. Healthy Pumpkin Muffins

Gluten-free and moist, these pumpkin muffins are an excellent breakfast fare on the go, especially during the fall season. On top, they are easy to make in the microwave.

Preparation Time: 5 Minutes
Cooking Time: 2 Minutes
Servings: 1
Ideal Size of the Mug: 12 oz.

Ingredients:

- 1 Egg (40gm), medium
- ½ tsp. or 0.85gm Pumpkin Pie Spice
- 1/3 cup or 75gm Pumpkin Puree
- 1 tsp. or 4.5gm Coconut Oil
- 3 tbsp. or 21gm Flaxseed Meal, grounded
- 1 ½ tsp. or 7gm Honey
- ¼ tsp. or 1.2gm Baking Powder
- Dash of Salt

Method of Preparation:

1) First, crack an egg into a greased microwave-safe bowl and whisk it with a fork.

2) After that, stir in all the remaining ingredients and give it a good mix until combined.

3) Place the mug into the microwave and heat on high heat for 1 to 2 minutes or until cooked. Once done, the muffins will rise slightly. Tip: Halfway through the cooking time, stir them and continue cooking. Allow it to cool for a minute or two after it is done.

4) To check whether it is done, insert a toothpick in the middle portion. It is done if the toothpick comes clean.

5) Serve it warm with butter or honey. Spreading nut butter like peanut butter or almond butter on top is also an excellent option.

Tips:

- Grease the mug with cooking oil spray.

- If the muffin batter overflows, turn off the microwave and let it sink down. Then continue heating in intervals.

- Top it with chopped nuts or whipped cream or berries.

- Instead of honey, you can use maple syrup.

- As the muffins are made with flax seed meal, they will not rise as much as ones made with flour.

Variations:

- To make it more nutritious, you can add a teaspoon of rolled old-fashioned oats to it. You can even top it with more oats.

Nutritional Information per serving:

- **Calories**: 281Kcal
- **Carbohydrates**: 22g
- **Fat**: 17g
- **Proteins:** 11g

7. Pancake Bowl

When pancake cravings set in, this recipe for pancake in a mug will come in handy. Furthermore, they are so delicious. Alongside, you don't have to stand by the side of your stove making batches of pancakes when all you want to do is make one or two.

Preparation Time: 5 Minutes
Cooking Time: 1 to 2 Minutes
Servings: 1
Ideal Size of the Mug: 12 oz.

Ingredients:

- 2 tbsp. or 24gm Sugar
- 4 tbsp. or 32gm All-Purpose Flour
- 1 tsp. or 4.2gm Vanilla extract
- ½ tsp. or 2.4gm Baking Powder
- 3 tbsp. or 45ml Milk of your choice
- 1 tbsp. or 14gm Butter, salted & melted

Method of Preparation:

1) To start with, grease a wide microwave-safe mug or bowl and place the dry ingredients in it. Whisk it with a fork.

2) Once combined, pour the liquid ingredients into it and give a good mix. Tip: The texture of the batter should be runny without any lumps.

3) Cook the mixture at high heat for 90 seconds while placing it in the center portion of the microwave. Tip: Or you can try heating for 60 seconds first and then cook in 10-seconds bursts until it is moist and set in the center.

4) Allow it to cool for a few minutes before serving.

5) Serve it warm and top it with butter, maple syrup, or berries.

Tips:

- Instead of butter, you can use applesauce, but the texture will be less fluffy. Or else use vegetable oil.

- It is possible to make the pancake in a mug with a store-bought pancake mix. Fill ¼ of the cup with the batter and cook until set.

- Instead of all-purpose flour, you can use cake flour, spelt flour, and gluten-free flour mix. Avoid low-carb flour.

- Milk can be substituted with water, but it will be less flavourful.

- Though not essential, place a paper towel under the mug to avoid spilling up.

- To make it protein-rich, add one tablespoon of protein powder and two tablespoons of flour to the batter.

- With regard to sugar, you can use regular or brown sugar.

Variations:

- If you want to make a chocolate chip pancake, add one teaspoon of chocolate chips to the batter.

Nutritional Information per serving:

- **Calories**: 366Kcal
- **Carbohydrates**: 50g
- **Fat**: 16g
- **Proteins:** 5g

8. French Toast

Simple to make yet full of flavor, this French toast made in a mug is as delightful as the usual ones.

Preparation Time: 5 Minutes
Cooking Time: 1 to 2 Minutes
Servings: 1

Ingredients:

- 2 Bread Slices (approx. 68gm)
- 3 tbsp. or 45ml Milk
- 1 Egg or 40gm, medium
- Drop of Vanilla Extract
- Pinch of Cinnamon, ground

Method of Preparation:

1) First, cube the bread and then pat the microwave-safe mug with butter. Tip: You can melt the butter and swish it around.

2) Next, place the bread cubes in it.

3) After that, combine milk, egg, vanilla extract, and cinnamon in another small bowl until mixed. Tip: Make sure there are no clumps of egg in it.

4) Pour this mixture into the cup and set it aside for a minute or two so that the liquid gets soaked by the bread. Stir well so that all the pieces are coated with the mixture evenly.

5) Now, heat it on high power for a minute. If needed, cook for another 10 seconds or continue in 10 seconds increments until it is cooked without any runny eggs.

6) Serve it warm and top it with maple syrup.

Tips:

- Any bread can be used for making this French toast. To make it healthier, you can go for multi-grain or sprouted bread.

- You can add toppings, like berries, banana slices, chocolate chips, whipped cream, peanut butter, etc., on top of it.

- Stale bread works the best for French toast. Avoid soft bread as it will make it mushy easily.

- Milk can be substituted with double cream to make it richer in taste. Almond milk and coconut milk are also excellent substitutes for milk.

- For more flavor, you can add a pinch of nutmeg.

- Do not stir the bread pieces vigorously.

- To make it vegan, use vegan butter, flax seeds, and non-dairy milk like almond milk.

Variation:

- To make it a savory French toast, combine the milk and egg with salt and pepper. After that, add your choice of meat, shredded cheese, and finely diced veggies into it. Stir well and add the bread cubes. Cook for 90 seconds or until the middle portion is set.

Nutritional Information per serving:

- **Calories**: 248Kcal
- **Carbohydrates**: 31g
- **Fat**: 7.4g
- **Proteins:** 13g

9. Banana Bread

Fluffy and moist, this banana bread can be made in less than 10 minutes, with just one ripe banana.

Preparation Time: 5 Minutes
Cooking Time: 1 to 2 Minutes
Servings: 1
Ideal Size of the Mug: 12 to 16 oz.

Ingredients:

- 1 tbsp. or 15ml Milk
- 1/8 tsp. Baking Powder
- 1 tbsp. or 12gm Sugar
- 1 Egg or 40gm, medium
- 1 Ripe Banana or 118 gm, mashed
- 2 tbsp. or 25gm Brown Sugar
- 1 tbsp. or 13.6gm Vegetable Oil
- 3 tbsp. or 27gm All-Purpose Flour
- ¼ tsp. or 1.5gm Vanilla Extract
- 1/8 tsp. Baking Soda
- Dash of Salt
- Chocolate chips, as needed, optional

Method of Preparation:

1) To start with, combine flour, baking soda, powder, brown sugar, salt, and sugar in a large-sized greased microwave mug with a whisker.

2) Add the egg to it, followed by oil, milk, mashed banana, and vanilla extract. Tip: Ensure the banana is mashed properly without any lumps in it.

3) Cook on high heat for 90 seconds first. Check the consistency and continue cooking in ten seconds increments or until it is done. Tip: When done, the cake's top will be set and firm to touch.

4) Set it aside for a few minutes before serving.

5) Serve warm and top it with ice cream, chocolate chips, or chocolate sauce if desired.

Tips:

- Choose the ripest banana. Riper the banana, more pronounced would be the banana flavor and sweetness.

- If you like crunchy textured cakes, add broken walnuts to them.

- Instead of bananas, you can use pineapple or blueberries.

- Do not overcook, as it will become dry and rubbery.

- Instead of vegetable oil, you can use any neutral oil.

- Fill the batter halfway through to ensure even cooking.

- To make it healthier, you can add one teaspoon of flax seeds to it.

Variation:

- If you wish to make chocolate banana bread, add 1 ½ teaspoon cocoa powder.

Nutritional Information per serving:

- **Calories**: 496Kcal
- **Carbohydrates**: 72g
- **Fat**: 20g
- **Proteins**: 11g

10. Cinnamon Roll

When you crave something sweet for your breakfast, this recipe for cinnamon roll will help you instantly by providing the classic flavor of your cinnamon roll without much effort and time.

Preparation Time: 5 Minutes
Cooking Time: 2 to 3 Minutes
Servings: 1
Ideal Size of the Mug: 12 oz.

Ingredients:

- 2 tbsp. or 16gm Flour
- ½ tsp. or 2.1gm Vanilla Extract
- 1 tsp. or 2.8gm Cinnamon, grounded
- 1 Egg or 40gm
- 1 tbsp. Coconut Oil or 13.6gm, melted
- Dash of Nutmeg
- 1 ½ tbsp. or 30gm Maple Syrup
- 1/8 tsp. Salt
- 2 tbsp. Milk or 30ml
- ½ tsp. or 2.4gm Baking Powder

For the icing:

- 1 tbsp. or 14gm Butter
- ½ tsp. or 2.4gm Lemon Juice
- 1 tbsp. or 15ml Milk
- 1 tsp. or 4.2gm Granulated Sugar

Method of Preparation:

1) First, combine all the ingredients needed to make the roll in a greased microwave-safe bowl. Add the baking powder last. Tip: The batter should be pretty loose while being thick.

2) After that, heat on high power for 2 minutes. Tip: When a toothpick inserted in the center comes clean, it's done. The top portion would be slightly soft and damp.

3) Mix all the ingredients needed for making the icing in another small bowl.

4) Drizzle the icing over the warm cinnamon roll.

5) Serve it warm.

Tips:

- Choose a medium or small-sized microwave mug for this. Taller mugs will result in a flatter cinnamon roll.

- Shredded coconut, jam, coconut chips, nuts, and sprinkles are excellent add-ins to the roll.

- Instead of maple syrup, you can use brown or coconut sugar.

Variations:

- Instead of combining all the ingredients in the mug, you can make the dough first by combining flour, baking powder, milk, sugar, vanilla, and butter. Flatten the dough and pour the butter, brown sugar, and cinnamon syrup over it. Roll into a cinnamon roll shape and place it in the mug.

Nutritional Information per serving:

- **Calories**: 452Kcal
- **Carbohydrates**: 39g
- **Fat**: 30g
- **Proteins:** 9g

LUNCH & DINNER

11. Lasagne in Mug

With layers of pasta, tomato sauce, and cheese, this microwave lasagne is a delight to enjoy!

Preparation Time: 5 Minutes

Cooking Time: 7 to 8 Minutes

Servings: 1

Ideal Size of the Mug: 16 oz.

Ingredients:

- ½ tbsp. or 0.6gm Basil, chopped
- ¼ cup or 50gm Cherry Tomatoes, halved
- 2 Lasagne Sheets or 66gm, roughly broken
- ¼ cup or 56.2gm Marinara Sauce
- ½ cup or 112gm Mozzarella Cheese, shredded & partly skimmed
- 1 tsp. or 4 gm Olive Oil
- ¼ of 1 Bell Pepper or 35gm, finely diced
- 1 ½ cup or 360ml Water, boiling

Method of Preparation:

1) First, place the lasagne noodles in a wide and tall microwave-safe mug, and then pour 1 ½ cups of water and 1 tsp. of olive oil into it. Tip: The water should cover the noodles. By adding oil to the water, you will be able to stop the lasagne from sticking together.

2) Next, place the mug onto a plate, so the liquid doesn't boil over while cooking the noodles.

3) Cook for 2 minutes and then stir.

4) Continue cooking for another two minutes. Tip: Check how much the pasta has cooked and whether it is tender.

5) Now, cook for two more minutes or until the lasagne is al dente. Tip: Reserve one tablespoon of the pasta liquid.

6) Then, stir in the chopped tomatoes, bell pepper, and marinara sauce. Top it with basil and shredded cheese.

7) Cover the mug with a paper towel and cook for 2 minutes. Tip: At this point, the cheese would have melted completely, and the lasagne heated through.

8) Serve it warm.

Tips:

- You can use any type of shredded cheese like parmesan or provolone.

- Add more herbs if desired for more freshness.

- Chopped sausage is another excellent add-in that can be added to this lasagne.

- To make it more nutritious, stir in ¼ cup of diced eggplant or chopped spinach.

Variations:

- Instead of using store-bought marinara sauce, you can make your base. Mix garlic, oregano, mushrooms, tomato, pepper, and salt. Add your choice of veggies and cook for 1 to 2 minutes or until they are tender. Now, add the noodles and cook as mentioned in the recipe.

Nutritional Information per serving:

- **Calories**: 384Kcal

- **Carbohydrates**: 52.7g

- **Fat**: 10.5g

- **Proteins:** 18.9g

12. Meatloaf in a Mug

Tender and juicy, this meatloaf in a mug is one that you can make with a few ingredients in 10 minutes.

Preparation Time: 5 Minutes
Cooking Time: 3 to 4 Minutes
Servings: 1
Ideal Size of the Mug: 16 oz.

Ingredients:

- 1 ½ tsp. or 1.3gm Taco Seasoning
- 4 oz. or 113gm Extra-lean ground beef
- 2 tbsp. Cilantro, fresh
- 2 tbsp. or 16gm Black Beans, drained & washed
- 2 tbsp. Salsa
- 2 tbsp. or 16gm Corn Kernels, cooked & softened
- 1 tbsp. or 10gm Oats, quick-cooking

Method of Preparation:

1) First, combine all the ingredients needed to make the meatloaf in a greased mug. Mix well. Smoothen it out evenly.

2) After that, heat on high power for 3 to 3 ½ minutes or until the meat is cooked. Tip: The temperature of the meat should be around 160 ° F and no longer be pink in color.

3) Set it aside to cool.

4) Serve warm.

Tips:

- Choose meat that has a higher ratio of fat to beef. This will ensure the meat doesn't get dried out during heat since it is cooked fast. A 70 to 30 blend would be an excellent choice.

- If preferred, you can top it with more tomato sauce.

- Instead of topping it with tomato sauce, you can glaze it with barbeque sauce.

- For a spicier version, you can use Picante sauce.

Variations:

- Another easy method would be to use an onion soup mix, ground beef, oats, ketchup, and milk. Mix soup mix, oats, ketchup, and milk in a bowl. To this, add the beef and stir well. Transfer the mixture to a mug and cook on high heat for 3 minutes or until the meat is no longer pink in color.

Nutritional Information per serving:

- **Calories**: 316Kcal
- **Carbohydrates**: 14g
- **Fat**: 14g
- **Proteins**: 33g

13. Mac & Cheese in a Mug

This easy recipe for mac and cheese is perfect for a single serving of your favorite comfort food. On top, it is as cheesy as you can get.

Preparation Time: 5 Minutes
Cooking Time: 4 to 5 Minutes
Servings: 1
Ideal Size of the Mug: 20 oz.

Ingredients:

- 4 tbsp. or 58.8gm Cheddar Cheese, finely shredded
- 1/3 cup or 31gm Elbow Macaroni
- ½ tsp. or 1.25gm Cornstarch
- Sea Salt, as needed
- ¾ cup or 175ml of Water
- 4 tbsp. or 6oml Milk of your choice
- Fresh Chives, for garnishing, as required

Method of Preparation:

1) Place the pasta, salt, and warm water in a large microwave-safe mug or bowl.

2) Keep the mug on a plate to avoid spill-up. Tip: While boiling, the water may rise and cause a spill.

3) After that, heat it on high power for 3 to 3 ½ minutes or until the pasta is cooked & moist. Tip: Stir well so that any macaroni stuck at the bottom gets loosened up. Check the pasta halfway through. If the pasta seems dry, add a bit more water. All the water should get absorbed by the time the pasta gets cooked. Cook them in intervals while having 2-minute intervals in between. Stir well during each break.

4) Remove the excess water.

5) Add the remaining ingredients and microwave them again for another minute. Tip: Make sure to add the rest of the ingredients immediately while the pasta is hot. The mix must be stirred for the first half minute if the pasta is cold.

6) The cheese mix should melt entirely and coat the pasta evenly.

7) Stir well and check for seasoning. Add more if desired. Garnish it with chives.

8) Serve it warm.

Tips:

- Elbow macaroni can be substituted with other short pasta like penne etc. But then, avoid large-shaped pasta.

- If desired, you can top the pasta with more cheese to make it cheesier and more flavourful.

- If the macaroni is not tender after cooking and all the water has been absorbed, add one more tablespoon of water or two to cook it further.

- Instead of cheddar cheese, you can use mozzarella cheese. Or you can use a combo of both kinds of cheese.

- In case the cheese and milk are beginning to get separated, make sure to lower the heat and cook.

- You can top it with crumbled bacon or jalapenos chopped.

- Instead of chives, you can use fresh parsley.

Variations:

- To make the dish vegan, use vegan cheese, nut milk, and desiccated coconut.

Nutritional Information per serving:

- **Calories**: 452Kcal
- **Carbohydrates**: 39g
- **Fat**: 30g
- **Proteins**: 9g

14. Potato Soup in a Mug

Though it has more ingredients than the other microwave meal recipes, this recipe for creamy potato soup is still quick and easy to make. Furthermore, the taste is totally oh so delicious while being satiating.

Preparation Time: 5 Minutes
Cooking Time: 5 to 7 Minutes
Servings: 1
Ideal Size of the Mug: 20 oz.

Ingredients:

- ¾ cup or 170ml of Water
- 1 tbsp. Bacon, chopped & cooked
- 3 tbsp. Potatoes (Approx half of 1 potato)
- 2 tsp. or 5gm Cornstarch
- ¼ cup or 60ml of Whole Milk
- ½ tbsp. or 7gm Butter
- 1 tbsp. or 18gm Onion

- Salt & Black Pepper, as needed
- 2 tbsp. or 59.4gm Cheddar Cheese
- ½ cup or 100ml Chicken Stock

Method of Preparation:

1) Begin by placing water and potato cubes in a large microwave-safe mug or bowl.

2) Cook for 3 to 4 minutes or until the potatoes are soft. Tip: Check halfway through the cooking time and stir well.

3) Once the potatoes are cooked, drain the excess water.

4) Add butter, half of the bacon, cheddar cheese, and onion to it. Mix well. Tip: Make sure the potatoes are warm while adding these ingredients.

5) Spoon in the cornstarch. Pour the chicken stock and milk into it. Stir well.

6) Check for seasoning and add more salt and pepper to it if desired.

7) Cook at high heat for 2 ½ to 3 minutes or until the soup has thickened.

8) Top it with the remaining bacon.

9) Serve it warm.

Tips:

- You can top it with sour cream and chives for more flavor.

- Though you can use any potatoes for this recipe, Yukon gold potatoes would be an excellent choice to consider.

- Instead of onion, you can use ½ tsp. of onion powder.

- If preferred, leek can be added.

Variations:

- To make the dish creamier, add evaporated milk and a tablespoon of water.

Nutritional Information per serving:

- **Calories:** 126Kcal

- **Carbohydrates**: 11g
- **Fat**: 7g
- **Proteins:** 6g

15. Pizza in a Mug

Perfect as a lunch & dinner fare, this single-serving of mug pizza is utterly satisfying and takes only five minutes to make.

Preparation Time: 5 Minutes

Cooking Time: 1 to 1 ½ Minutes

Servings: 1

Ideal Size of the Mug: 16 oz.

Ingredients:

- 1 ½ tbsp. or 27gm Mozzarella Cheese, grated
- 3 tbsp. or 24gm All-Purpose Flour
- Dash of Salt
- 1 ½ tbsp. or 21gm Tomato Pasta Sauce
- 1 tbsp. or 13gm Olive Oil
- 1/8 tsp. Baking Soda
- Pinch of Baking Powder
- 3 tbsp. or 45ml Milk

- ½ of 1 or Pepperoni Stick or Pepperoni, sliced into rounds
- Dried Oregano, as required

Method of Preparation:

1) To start with, place flour, salt, baking powder, and soda in a greased and floured microwave-safe bowl or mug. Stir well.

2) After that, pour the milk and olive oil into it.

3) Give a good stir until everything comes together. Tip: There would be a few lumps here and there.

4) Then, top it with the tomato pasta sauce and garnish it with the cheese. Sprinkle oregano on top.

5) Heat it on high heat for 1 minute or until cooked. Tip: The topping will start bubbling, and the edges will begin crisping up.

6) Remove it from the microwave and top it with the pepperoni sticks. Heat it further for 20 to 30 seconds. Allow it to cool for a few minutes before serving.

7) Serve it warm

Tips:

- You can top it with fresh herbs like basil or oregano for more flavor.
- Garlic powder and onion powder can be added for more taste.
- Tomato sauce can be substituted with marinara sauce.
- Instead of oregano, you can use dried Italian seasoning.
- To spice it up, you can top it with dried chili flakes.

Nutritional Information per serving:

- **Calories**: 342Kcal
- **Carbohydrates**: 27g
- **Fat**: 20g
- **Proteins**: 10g

16. Chicken Stew in a Mug

With tender chicken and savory veggies, this chicken stew is an easy shortcut to the classic one.

Preparation Time: 5 Minutes

Cooking Time: 6 Minutes

Servings: 1

Ideal Size of the Mug: 16 oz.

Ingredients:

- 100gm Cooked Chicken, shredded
- ½ of 1 Onion or 26gm, finely chopped
- ½ of 1 Leek Stalk, finely chopped
- ½ of 1 Potato or 70gm, small & finely cubed
- ½ of 1 Carrot or 25gm, finely diced
- ½ tsp. Fresh Herbs, as desired
- 2 tbsp. or 6gm Chicken Stock
- 2 tbsp. or 6gm Chicken Stock Granules

Method of Preparation:

1) To start with, pour the chicken stock into the mug and then add the onion, carrot, leek, and potatoes into it.

2) After that, place it in the microwave and cook for 2 minutes at high heat. Cover it with plastic wrap and pierce it with a fork to make holes. Place a plate below the mug.

3) Once 2 minutes is up, take out the mug and stir well. Continue to cook for further 2 minutes or until the veggies are tender.

4) Now, add all the remaining ingredients to the mug and combine well.

5) Cook again for another 2 minutes or until it comes together.

6) Set it aside for a few minutes before serving.

7) Serve it warm.

Tips:

- You can top it with fresh herbs like basil or oregano for more flavor.

- Garlic powder and onion powder can be added for more taste.

- Instead of onion, you can use ½ tsp. of onion powder.

- If you wish to make it spicier, add coarsely crushed peppercorns

- To make it more nutritious, you can add quinoa to it.

- You can add your choice of root veggies into it.

Nutritional Information per serving:

- **Calories**: 320Kcal
- **Carbohydrates**: 24.4g
- **Fat**: 5.2g
- **Proteins:** 43.5g

17. Risotto in a Mug

This simple single-serving recipe for cheesy and creamy risotto can be made quickly in the microwave.

Preparation Time: 5 Minutes

Cooking Time: 10 Minutes

Servings: 1

Ideal Size of the Mug: 14 oz.

Ingredients:

- 1 tbsp. or 14gm Butter
- 1/3 cup or approx. 50gm. Arborio Rice
- 1 tbsp. or 18gm Onion, finely chopped
- 20ml White Wine
- ½ of 1 Garlic, finely minced
- ½ cup or approx. 80ml Chicken Broth
- Pinch of Dried Thyme
- 1 tbsp. or 14 gm Parmesan Cheese, shredded

Method of Preparation:

1) First, add the butter and the onion to a large microwave-safe mug or bowl.

2) Heat it for 60 seconds on high heat, and once the butter has melted and the onion has softened, spoon in the garlic, dried thyme, rice, and stock to it. Combine.

3) Cover it with plastic wrap and pierce holes with a fork.

4) Cook for 4 minutes on medium heat.

5) Take the mug from the microwave and stir well. Add more broth if necessary and cook for another 4 minutes.

6) Next, pour the wine into it and stir. Top it with the parmesan. Cook for further 2 minutes or until the rice is cooked.

7) Set it aside for a few minutes before serving.

8) Serve it warm.

Tips:

- You can drizzle olive oil at the end if desired.

- To make pumpkin risotto, add 60gm cubed butternut pumpkin to it.

- You can garnish it with mint leaves to enhance the flavor.

- For a mushroom-flavored risotto, soak dried porcini mushrooms in a cup of chicken broth. Heat on high heat for 1 minute and set it aside for 4 minutes. Remove the mushroom pieces. Now, add the chicken- mushroom stock to the mug.

Variation:

- For a change, add cooked bacon, kale, parmesan cheese, and mushrooms into it. Once the rice is cooked, you can add mushrooms to it before adding stock. Then, add kale and cooked bacon to it. Heat for 60 seconds on high heat, and finally add parmesan cheese.

Nutritional Information per serving:

- **Calories**: 403Kcal
- **Carbohydrates**: 68.1g
- **Fat**: 9.1g
- **Proteins:** 7.6g

18. Fried Rice in a Mug

Have you thought it is possible to make fried rice in the microwave and that too within five to ten minutes? So here comes the tasty and simple recipe.

Preparation Time: 5 Minutes
Cooking Time: 10 Minutes
Servings: 1

Ingredients:

- ½ cup or 100gm Jasmine Rice
- 1 cup or 100ml of Water
- ½ tsp. or 1gm Onion Powder
- 2 tbsp. or 16gm Peas
- ¼ tsp. or 2.5gm Five-Spice Powder
- 2 tbsp. or 30gm Red Pepper, chopped
- ½ tsp. or 2.25gm Sesame Oil
- ½ of 1 Stalk of Green Onion
- 1 tbsp. or 16.6gm Soy Sauce

- 1 Egg, medium (40gm)
- A bit of Sliced Cabbage & Sprouts

Method of Preparation:

1) To start with, place rice, water, soya sauce, and sesame oil in a greased microwave-safe bowl.

2) Cover the cup with plastic wrap and pierce it with a fork to make a few holes.

3) Heat the mix for 4 minutes on high heat.

4) Stir and continue cooking for another 4 minutes.

5) In the meantime, combine egg, onion powder, five-spice powder, and green onion to it.

6) Pour the egg mixture into the mug and stir well. Add peas, cabbage, sprouts, and red pepper.

7) Cover it with plastic wrap and cook for 90 to 120 seconds. Tip: The vegetables should be crisp-tender.

8) Set it aside for a few minutes before serving.

9) Serve it warm.

Tips:

- You can garnish it with scallions if desired.
- Another excellent add-in would be the addition of cooked bacon.
- Instead of Jasmine rice, you can use any long grain rice.
- For more flavor, you can try adding either tomato sauce or teriyaki sauce.
- To make it spicier, you can spoon in sriracha sauce or chili oil.
- For a low-carb version of fried rice, use riced cauliflower instead of Jasmine rice.

Variation:

- You can also make fried rice in a mug with instant ready-to-serve rice. For this, you would need to whisk the egg in a separate bowl. Cook for one minute on high heat and break it into smaller pieces. Then, cook the veggies for another 1 minute. Finally, heat the rice for one minute and spoon in the sauce. Mix the rice, veggies, and egg. Serve warm.

Nutritional Information per serving:

- **Calories**: 344Kcal
- **Carbohydrates**: 53g
- **Fat**: 9.1g
- **Proteins:** 15g

19. Meatball Stew in a Mug

One of my favorite things on earth is meatball stew, and this recipe made in a mug does not take more than 10 to 15 minutes to make it. What more can we ask for?

Preparation Time: 5 Minutes
Cooking Time: 7 to 8 Minutes
Servings: 1
Ideal Size of the Mug: 16 to 20 oz.

Ingredients:

- Sea Salt & Black Pepper, as needed
- 2 tbsp. jarred Mushroom Slices
- ½ cup or 125mg Marinara Sauce
- 1/3 cup or 75gm Mixed Vegetables, cooked
- 1/3 cup or 75ml Chicken Stock

For the meatballs:

- ¼ lb. Ground Beef
- ½ of 1 Egg (20gm)
- Sea Salt & Black Pepper, as needed
- ¼ cup or 30gm Bread Crumbs
- 1 Garlic clove or 4 gm, finely minced
- 3 tbsp. or 45ml Milk
- 3 tbsp. or 45gm Parmesan Cheese, grated

Method of Preparation:

1) First, combine all the ingredients needed to make the meatball in a bowl and mix well.

2) Make balls out of this meat dough. Tip: Oil your hand before making the meatballs.

3) Place the meatballs on the greased microwave-safe plate and cook on high heat for four minutes. Tip: Check halfway through the cooking time.

4) Flip them once and cook for another 2 minutes.

5) Once done, cut the meatballs in half. Tip: The internal temperature of the meatballs should be around 165 ° F, and the meat should no longer be pink in color.

6) After that, place the meatballs, marinara sauce, mushrooms, mixed vegetables, and broth in a large mug. Mix well.

7) Cook for another 2 minutes or until it is heated through.

8) Check for seasoning and add more salt and pepper as desired.

9) Set it aside for a few minutes before serving.

10) Serve it warm.

Tips:

- Instead of chicken broth, you can use vegetable broth.

- Instead of meatballs, you can use vegetarian balls.

- Ground beef can be substituted by meatloaf mix.

- Instead of bread crumbs, you can use quinoa or grains.

- For more flavor, you can add Worcestershire sauce to it.

Variation:

- Another option would be to use ready-to-use meatballs, which need to be heated for 4 minutes on high heat in the microwave.

Nutritional Information per serving:

- **Calories**: 333Kcal

- **Carbohydrates**: 29g
- **Fat**: 14g
- **Proteins:** 22g

20. Chicken Pot Pie in a Mug

The ultimate comfort dish that can be made in a cup and that too in a snap!

Preparation Time: 5 Minutes

Cooking Time: 2 to 3 Minutes

Servings: 1

Ideal Size of the Mug: 12 oz.

Ingredients:

- ½ cup or 85gm Mixed vegetables
- 4 tbsp. Cooked Chicken, diced
- ¼ tsp. or 0.35gm Dried Thyme
- 3 Phyllo Cups
- Kosher Salt & freshly grounded Black Pepper, as needed
- 1 tsp. or 3.3gm Flour
- ¼ cup or 60ml of Milk
- 1 tbsp. or 14gm Butter

Method of Preparation:

1) To start with, place the butter on the bottom of the microwave-safe mug or bowl and then add the vegetables to it. Sprinkle the dried thyme over it.

2) Cook on high heat for 1 minute.

3) In the meantime, soak the phyllo cups in milk in another bowl.

4) Then, spoon the flour and milk into the bowl or mug.

5) Stir the mixture well until they are no more lumps.

6) Next, add the chicken, salt, and pepper to it. Stir well.

7) Now, cook for a further 2 minutes or until the chicken is heated through.

8) Once done, crumble the phyllo cups and sprinkle them on top.

9) Check for seasoning and add more salt and pepper as desired.

10) Set it aside for a few minutes before serving.

11) Serve it warm.

Tips:

- Instead of chicken, you can use any meat.

- The phyllo cups can be substituted with pre-made pie crust. Cut the crust in the shape of the mug and use it.

- Crescent rolls are also an excellent option to consider as a topping.

- Cream can be added to make it richer.

- Instead of using flour, you can use cornstarch.

Variation:

- Another option would be to use ready-to-use meatballs, which need to be heated for 4 minutes on high heat in the microwave.

Nutritional Information per serving:

- **Calories**: 428Kcal

- **Carbohydrates**: 35g

- **Fat**: 13g
- **Proteins:** 42g

MUG CAKES

21. Peanut Butter Mug Cake

Love chocolate? Love peanut butter? Then here comes a moist chocolate cake that combines your two loves and that you can make in two minutes.

Preparation Time: 5 Minutes

Cooking Time: 1 to 2 Minutes

Servings: 1

Ideal Size of the Mug: 12oz.

Ingredients:

- 3 tbsp. or 24gm All-Purpose Flour
- 2 tbsp. or 30gm Peanut Butter
- ¼ tsp. or 1.2gm Baking Powder
- 2 tbsp. or 24gm Sugar
- 1 ½ tbsp. or 21gm Butter, melted
- 1 ½ tbsp. or 10gm Cocoa Powder, unsweetened
- Dash of Sea Salt
- 3 tbsp. or 45ml Milk

Method of Preparation:

1) First, combine flour, salt, cocoa powder, sugar, and baking powder in the mug.

2) After that, pour milk, melted butter, and peanut butter into it. Stir well until you get a smooth batter.

3) Now, cook on high heat for one minute

4) Set it aside for a few minutes before serving.

5) Serve and enjoy.

Tips:

- For crunchiness, you can add chopped walnuts.

- Marshmallows are also a good choice as add-ins.

- You can add a teaspoon of applesauce to make it moister.

- Chocolate chips can be added for more chocolate flavor.

- Serve it along with ice cream or powdered sugar.

Variation:

- Instead of using peanut butter, you can use any nut butter like almond butter or nut butter.

Nutritional Information per serving:

- **Calories**: 512Kcal

- **Carbohydrates**: 54g

- **Fat**: 30g

- **Proteins:** 9g

22. Peach Cobbler Mug Cake

With buttery peaches and hints of vanilla and cardamon, this peach cobbler made in a mug is truly delicious.

Preparation Time: 5 Minutes
Cooking Time: 3 Minutes
Servings: 1
Ideal Size of the Mug: 12oz.

Ingredients:

- 3 tbsp. or 37.5gm Brown Sugar, lite
- ¼ tsp. or 1.2gm Baking Powder
- 1 ½ cup or 240gm Peaches, frozen
- ¼ tsp. or 1.5gm Vanilla Extract
- 1 tbsp. or 14gm Butter
- 1 tbsp. Sugar or 12gm, granulated
- 1 tsp. Cinnamon or 2.8gm, grounded
- 2 tbsp. or 30ml Milk
- 2 tbsp. All-Purpose Flour or 16gm
- Dash of Salt

Method of Preparation:

1) Begin by placing peaches, brown sugar, and half of the ground cinnamon in a bowl.

2) Heat the mixture for 1 ½ minute or until the peaches are defrosted. Stir well.

3) After that, melt the butter in a microwave-safe mug by heating it for 30 seconds on high heat.

4) Once melted, pour the peach mixture over it and keep it aside.

5) Mix flour, salt, remaining cinnamon, baking powder, sugar, vanilla extract, and milk in another bowl of milk. Mix well.

6) Pour this mixture over the peach mixture.

7) Finally, cook on high heat for 1 minute or until it is cooked.

8) Garnish it with more brown sugar if desired.

9) Set it aside for a few minutes before serving.

10) Serve and enjoy.

Tips:

- If using fresh peaches, cook them a little longer as they are slightly harder.

- Instead of using peaches, you can use mixed berries and cherries.

- Instead of brown sugar, you can use turbinado sugar.

- The cobbler pairs well with vanilla ice cream.

- For making the vegan version, use vegan butter and nut milk.

Variation:

- Instead of using flour, you can use cake mix.

Nutritional Information per serving:

- **Calories**: 512Kcal
- **Carbohydrates**: 54g
- **Fat**: 30g
- **Proteins**: 9g

23. Pumpkin Cheese Cake

Tender, rich and moist, this winter dessert can be easily made in the microwave.

Preparation Time: 5 Minutes
Cooking Time: 1 to 2 Minutes
Servings: 1
Ideal Size of the Mug: 12oz.

Ingredients:

- 1 tsp. or 4.2gm Vanilla Extract
- 1 tbsp. Pumpkin Puree
- 2 tbsp. or 30gm Yogurt, unsweetened
- 1 tsp. Pumpkin Pie Spice Mix
- 1 tbsp. or 12gm Sweetener, granulated
- ½ tsp. or 2.4gm Baking Powder
- ¼ cup or 55gm Cream Cheese

Method of Preparation:

1) To start with, place the cream cheese in the greased microwave-safe mug and heat it for 3 seconds on high heat or until softened. Tips: Ensure that they are no lumps in it.

2) Now, add all the remaining ingredients to it and mix well.

3) Then, cook on medium heat for 1 minute. Heat again for a further 1 minute. Do not cook the entire 2 minutes in one stretch as it will cause the cream cheese to become unstable and explode. Tip: At this point, the top portion is set, and the edges start pulling away from the mug's sides.

4) Set it aside for 10 minutes. Garnish it with pumpkin pie spice if desired.

5) Once cooled, place in the refrigerator for an hour.

6) Serve and enjoy.

Tips:

- Serve it with whipped cream or caramel sauce.

- Make sure to remove all moisture from the pumpkin puree.

- You can add chocolate chips to it if desired.

- Instead of pumpkin spice mix, add ¼ teaspoon of nutmeg and cinnamon.

- Instead of granulated sugar, you can use erythritol.

Nutritional Information per serving:

- **Calories**: 249Kcal

- **Carbohydrates**: 7g

- **Fat**: 20.9g

- **Proteins:** 6.9g

24. Oatmeal Cookie Dough Cake

Soft and delicious cookie dough cookie that is healthy comes your way through this easy recipe. Make it, eat it, and love it!

Preparation Time: 5 Minutes
Cooking Time: 1 to 2 Minutes
Servings: 1
Ideal Size of the Mug: 12oz.

Ingredients:

- 2 tbsp. or 10gm Oats, quick cooking
- 1 tbsp. or 15gm Chocolate Chips
- ¼ tsp or 1.2gm Baking Powder
- 1 Egg White
- 3 tbsp. or 45ml Milk of your choice
- 1 ½ tbsp. or 10gm Coconut Flour
- 1 tbsp. or 12.5gm Brown Sugar

Method of Preparation:

1) First, place coconut flour, baking powder, and oats in a large microwave-safe bowl and mix it well.

2) To this, add milk and sugar. Stir well until they are no more lumps.

3) After that, stir in the egg white and whisk it well with a fork until well combined.

4) Now, spoon in the chocolate chips while reserving a few to top the cookie.

5) Finally, heat on high heat for 1 ½ to 2 minutes or until cooked. Tip: If it seems uncooked, continue cooking in 30-second increments until it is cooked to your desired consistency.

6) Serve and enjoy.

Tips:

- If preferred, add vanilla extract to it for more flavor.

- For a chewier texture, you can use old-fashioned oats.

- Dried cherries and raisins are excellent add-ins for the cookie.

- If desired, add a pinch of ground cinnamon for warm flavors.

Nutritional Information per serving:

- **Calories**: 183Kcal
- **Carbohydrates**: 30g
- **Fat**: 4.6g
- **Proteins:** 6.9g

25. Coffee Mug Cake

This coffee mug cake is a delicious treat that you nibble through when you want something sweet to satisfy your cravings.

Preparation Time: 5 Minutes
Cooking Time: 1 to 2 Minutes
Servings: 1
Ideal Size of the Mug: 12oz.

Ingredients:

- 1 tbsp. or 12gm Sugar, granulated
- ½ tbsp. or 6.25gm Brown Sugar
- 2 ½ tbsp. or 24gm All-Purpose Flour
- ¼ tsp. or 0.7gm Cinnamon, grounded
- Pinch of Salt
- 1 drop of Vanilla Extract
- 1 tbsp. or 15ml Almond Milk
- ¼ tsp. or 1.2gm Baking Powder
- 1 tbsp. or 13.6gm Vegetable Oil

Method of Preparation:

1) To begin with, place flour, vanilla extract, baking powder, salt, sugar, oil, and milk in it. Combine well.

2) Next, sprinkle brown sugar and cinnamon on top.

3) Heat on high heat for 45 seconds or until cooked. If not cooked, continue cooking in 15-seconds increments.

4) Allow it to cool for a few minutes before serving.

5) Serve and enjoy.

Tips:

- For a crunchy texture, you can try adding nuts like chopped almonds and pecan to it.

- For a much crispier topping, combine flour, cinnamon, brown sugar, and butter in a small bowl and then top it over the cake mix.

- Instead of all-purpose flour, you can use spelt flour, oat flour, or almond flour.

- Instead of oil, you can add applesauce.

- On top of the toppings, you can sprinkle powdered sugar glaze.

Nutritional Information per serving:

- **Calories**: 267Kcal
- **Carbohydrates**: 35g
- **Fat**: 14g
- **Proteins:** 2g

26. Honey Mug Cake

Honey mug cake is a gooey mug cake with the texture of pudding with a unique taste and flavor. Try it, and you are sure to get hooked.

Preparation Time: 5 Minutes
Cooking Time: 1 to 2 Minutes
Servings: 1
Ideal Size of the Mug: 12oz.

Ingredients:

- 2 tbsp. or 28gm Butter
- Dash of Salt
- 2 tbsp. or 42gm Honey, runny
- 4 tbsp. or 32gm Self-Rising Flour
- ½ tsp. or 2.1 Vanilla Extract
- 1 Egg or 40gm
- 3 tbsp. or 37.5gm Light Brown Sugar

For the frosting:

- 2 tbsp. or 28gm Butter, at room temperature
- 4 tbsp. or 28gmConfectioner's Sugar

Method of Preparation:

1) To begin with, place the butter in a large microwave-safe mug and heat it for 30 seconds or until melted.

2) After that, mix honey, vanilla extract, and egg into it with a fork until combined well.

3) Next, stir sugar, salt, and flour into it.

4) Give a good stir until everything comes together. The mixture should be smooth.

5) Heat on medium heat for 1 ½ minute or until cooked.

6) Allow it to cool for a few minutes before serving.

7) In the meantime, to make the frosting, mix the softened butter and confectioners' sugar in another bowl until you get a clumpy texture.

8) Now, whisk it with a fork for 1 to 2 minutes or until it becomes fluffy.

9) Transfer the frosting to a small piping bag and swirl the piping onto the top of the mug cake.

10) Drizzle with extra honey if desired.

11) Serve and enjoy.

Tips:

- Instead of self-rising flour, you can use a combo of all-purpose flour and ¼ tsp. baking powder.

- You can top it with whipping cream and sprinkles.

- A pinch of cinnamon powder can enhance the flavor of the mug cake since honey and cinnamon go well together.

- Another excellent add-in that can be used in this recipe is pumpkin spice powder.

Nutritional Information per serving:

- **Calories**: 381Kcal
- **Carbohydrates**: 61.7g
- **Fat**: 13.1g
- **Proteins**: 4.9g

27. S'mores Mug Cake

With gooey toasted marshmallows on top and crushed graham crackers inside, this quick fix is so tasty and delightful!

Preparation Time: 5 Minutes
Cooking Time: 2 Minutes
Servings: 1
Ideal Size of the Mug: 12oz.

Ingredients:

- 4 or 56gm Graham Crackers
- 1 Egg, large (56gm)
- 1 tbsp. or 14gm Butter softened
- 2 tbsp. or 16gm All-Purpose Flour
- 2 Jumbo Marshmallows or 14gm
- ¼ cup or 60ml Milk, whole
- Pinch of Baking Powder
- 1 oz. or 28gm Milk Chocolate
- 2 tbsp. or 24gm Sugar, granulated
- Dash of Salt

Method of Preparation:

1) To start with, crush the graham crackers in a Ziplock bag with the help of a rolling pin. Reserve a small portion for topping.

2) Mix flour, baking powder, crushed graham crackers, salt, and sugar in a large microwave-safe bowl.

3) To this, pour milk, butter, and egg. Whisk well with a fork until everything comes together.

4) Heat the mixture for 2 minutes on high heat.

5) Once done, top it with the milk chocolate and marshmallow. Heat for a further 1 minute or until the chocolate is melted.

6) Finally, top it with the reserved crushed graham crackers.

7) Serve and enjoy.

Tips:

- If preferred, you can add ground cinnamon to enhance the flavor.

- You can toast the marshmallows with a kitchen blow torch if desired.

- Serve it with vanilla ice cream.

- For more chocolatey flavor, you can add cocoa powder.

- If you prefer a hint of vanilla, add a drop of vanilla extract.

Nutritional Information per serving:

- **Calories**: 737Kcal
- **Carbohydrates**: 121g
- **Fat**: 21g
- **Proteins**: 16g

28. Gingerbread Mug Cake

Moist and boldly flavoured, this gingerbread mug cake is totally scrumptious.

Preparation Time: 5 Minutes
Cooking Time: 2 Minutes
Servings: 1
Ideal Size of the Mug: 12oz.

Ingredients:

- ¼ cup or 34gm All-Purpose Flour
- 1 ½ or 21gm tbsp. Butter
- Dash of Salt & Black Pepper
- ¼ tsp. or 0.6gm Ginger grounded
- 2 tbsp. or 24gm Sugar
- ¼ tsp. or 0.7gm Cinnamon, grounded
- 1 tbsp. or 17.5gm Molasses
- ¼ tsp. or 1.2gm Baking Powder
- 2 tbsp. or 30ml Milk
- 1/8 tsp. Vanilla Extract

Method of Preparation:

1) First, melt the butter in a large-microwave mug by heating it for 30 seconds on high heat. Swirl it around.

2) After that, combine molasses, sugar, vanilla extract, and milk in another bowl until mixed well.

3) Next, mix the remaining ingredients in the microwave until combined.

4) To this, pour the milk mixture and stir it until just combined.

5) Heat it for 60 to 90 seconds or until cooked.

6) Serve and enjoy.

Tips:

- Dust it with powdered sugar or top it with whipping cream.

- Instead of butter, you can also use vegetable oil.

- Both brown and white sugar goes well in this recipe.

- Instead of all-purpose flour, you can combine almond flour and coconut flour.

- Top it with sliced fruits like apples and pears to make it more nutritious.

Nutritional Information per serving:

- **Calories**: 315Kcal
- **Carbohydrates**: 45g
- **Fat**: 7g
- **Proteins:** 8.5g

29. Snickerdoodle Mug Cake

A decadent dessert that even the kids can easily make in the microwave.

Preparation Time: 5 Minutes
Cooking Time: 2 Minutes
Servings: 1
Ideal Size of the Mug: 14 oz.

Ingredients:

- ¼ cup or 32gm All-Purpose Flour
- ½ tsp. or 2.1gm Vanilla Extract
- 2 tbsp. or 24gm Sugar
- 2 tbsp. or 28gm Butter, salted & melted
- ¼ tsp. or 1.2gm Baking Powder
- ¼ cup or 60ml Milk
- ¼ tsp. or 0.7gm. Cinnamon, grounded
- Dash of Salt

For the topping:

- 1/4 tsp. or 0.7gm Cinnamon, grounded
- 1 tbsp. or 12gm Sugar

Method of Preparation:

1) To begin with, combine flour, cinnamon, salt, baking powder, and sugar in a large- microwave-safe bowl until no streaks remain.

2) To this, pour in milk, vanilla extract, and butter, and whisk it with a fork until you get a smooth batter.

3) Next, transfer the milk mixture to the nut mix. Mix well.

4) Then, combine sugar and cinnamon for the topping. Alternate between these two layers if desired.

5) Heat on high heat for 60 to 90 seconds or until the cake is cooked to your desired consistency. Tip: The top of the cake would be cooked and slightly sticky in the middle portion.

6) Allow it to cool for a few minutes.

7) Top the mug cake with more cinnamon sugar.

8) Serve and enjoy.

Tips:

- You can either use skim milk or whole milk. It is also possible to substitute it with nut milks also.

- Instead of butter, you can use oil though butter lends a better flavor. Another option would be to use applesauce.

- You can use white or brown sugar for this recipe.

- If preferred, top it with whipped cream or vanilla ice cream.

Nutritional Information per serving:

- **Calories**: 500Kcal
- **Carbohydrates**: 64g
- **Fat**: 25g
- **Proteins**: 5g

30. Caramel Macchiato Mug Cake

A highly decadent and lip-smacking mug cake that will satiate all your taste buds.

Preparation Time: 5 Minutes

Cooking Time: 2 Minutes

Servings: 1

Ideal Size of the Mug: 12oz.

Ingredients:

- ¾ tsp. or 3.6gm Baking Powder
- 3 tbsp. or 45ml Milk
- Dash of Salt
- 1 tbsp. or 28gm Caramel Sauce
- 1 ½ tsp. Instant Coffee Powder
- 1 tsp. or 4.2gm Vanilla Extract
- 2 tbsp. or 24gm Sugar, granulated
- 5 tbsp. or 4gm All-Purpose Flour
- 1 ½ tbsp. or 20gm Vegetable Oil

Method of Preparation:

1) To start with, mix all the dry ingredients in a large microwave-safe bowl.

2) Then, add the liquid ingredients and whisk them with a fork until everything comes together and is smooth.

3) Cook for 1 to 1 ½ minute or until the cake is cooked.

4) Allow it to cool for a few minutes before serving.

5) Serve and enjoy.

Tips:

- Top it with whipped cream and extra caramel sauce.

Nutritional Information per serving:

- **Calories**: 611Kcal
- **Carbohydrates**: 96g
- **Fat**: 23g
- **Proteins:** 7g

31. Healthy Carrot Mug Cake

A mug cake that is really good for you.

Preparation Time: 5 Minutes
Cooking Time: 2 Minutes
Servings: 1
Ideal Size of the Mug: 12oz.

Ingredients:

- Pinch of Sea Salt
- 1/3 cup or 41.8gm Oat Flour
- 1 tbsp. or 13.6gm Coconut Oil, melted
- ½ tsp. or 1.2gm Baking Powder
- 1 Egg or 40gm
- 3 tbsp. or 10gm Carrots, shredded
- ½ tsp. or 1.4gm Cinnamon, grounded
- 1 tbsp. or 17.5gm Molasses
- ½ tsp. or 2.1gm Vanilla Extract

Method of Preparation:

1) To start with, combine oat flour, baking powder, cinnamon, and salt in a large microwave-safe bowl.

2) Next, stir in egg, coconut oil, grated carrots, molasses, and vanilla extract to it.

3) Give a good mix until everything comes together.

4) Cook for 1 ½ minute or until the cake is set.

5) Allow it to cool for a few minutes.

6) Serve and enjoy.

Tips:

- You can butter instead of coconut oil.

- Oats flour can be substituted with whole wheat flour.

- Instead of molasses, you can use maple syrup.

- To get a crunchy texture inside, you can put raisins and dates

- For a crunchy topping, you can add chopped walnuts.

- If preferred, top it with cinnamon whipped cream, coconut flakes, or cream cheese frosting.

Nutritional Information per serving:

- **Calories**: 425Kcal
- **Carbohydrates**: 47g
- **Fat**: 22g
- **Proteins:** 12g

32. Coconut Mug Cake

For coconut lovers, here comes a moist & soft mug cake with a triple hit of coconut flavors.

Preparation Time: 5 Minutes

Cooking Time: 5 Minutes

Servings: 1

Size of the mug: 16 oz.

Ingredients:

- 1 tbsp. or 13.5gm Coconut Oil
- 1 tbsp. or 8gm Coconut Flakes, sweetened
- ½ tbsp. or 7.6gm Vegetable Oil
- ½ tsp. or 1.2gm Baking Powder
- 2 tbsp. or 30gm Coconut Milk, canned
- 2 ½ tbsp. or 35ml Milk, fat-free
- 4 tsp. or 20gm Sugar, granulated
- 6 or 48gm tbsp. All-Purpose Flour

Method of Preparation:

1) Start by melting the coconut oil in a large microwave-safe mug by heating it for 20-seconds.

2) After that, stir in coconut milk, vegetable oil, and milk into it. Whisk it with a fork until it becomes a smooth paste.

3) Then, add flour, baking powder, and sugar to it. Stir well until everything comes together.

4) Next, spoon the coconut flakes into it and mix well.

5) Heat it for 1 to 1 ½ minutes or until the cake is set.

6) Allow it to cool for a few minutes before serving.

7) Serve and enjoy.

Tips:

- Top it with whipped cream and toasted coconut flakes.

- To enhance the flavor, you can add coconut extract to it.

- Instead of sugar, you can use honey, maple, or agave syrup.

- If you want to reduce sweetness, you can use unsweetened coconut flakes.

Nutritional Information per serving:

- **Calories**: 488Kcal
- **Carbohydrates**: 58g
- **Fat**: 27g
- **Proteins:** 6g

33. Keto Lemon Mug Cake

Sweet & slightly start, this light, fluffy lemon cake is another sweet treat that you can make easily in the microwave.

Preparation Time: 5 Minutes
Cooking Time: 2 Minutes
Servings: 1
Ideal Size of the Mug: 12oz.

Ingredients:

- 2 tbsp. or 30gm Lemon Curd
- 2 tbsp. or 14gm Coconut Flour
- 1 tsp. or 2gm Lemon Zest
- 1 tbsp. or 12gm Sugar, granulated
- 1 Egg or 40gm
- 1 tbsp. or 14gm Butter, melted
- ¼ tsp. or 1.2gm Baking Powder
- 2 tbsp. or 22gm Cream Cheese
- 1 tsp. or 4.2gm Vanilla Extract

Method of Preparation:

1) To start with, mix cream cheese and butter in a large microwave-safe bowl until combined well.

2) Heat on high heat for 20 seconds.

3) Now, add all the remaining ingredients, excluding the lemon curd, to it, and give a good stir.

4) Then, spoon in the lemon curd. With the back of the spoon, push the curd into the cake batter so that it gets into the middle portion.

5) Finally, cook for 90 to 100 seconds or until cooked.

6) Serve and enjoy.

Tips:

- If desired, you can top it with a lemon sugar glaze. For this, combine 2 tablespoons of confectioners' sugar with ½ teaspoon lemon juice. For more flavor, you can add less than a drop of vanilla extract to it.

Nutritional Information per serving:

- **Calories**: 357Kcal
- **Carbohydrates**: 5.9g
- **Fat**: 32.6g
- **Proteins**: 14.4g

34. Red Velvet in a Mug

Light, moist and fluffy, this red velvet mug cake with hints of cocoa is healthy while being scrumptious.

Preparation Time: 2 Minutes
Cooking Time: 2 to 3 Minutes
Servings: 1
Ideal Size of the Mug: 12oz.

Ingredients:

- 1 ½ tbsp. or 10gm Coconut Flour
- ½ tsp. or 2.4gm Baking Powder
- 1 tbsp. or 6gm Almond Flour
- 1 Egg White
- ¼ cup or 60ml Milk
- Dash of Sea Salt
- 1 tbsp. or 12gm Sugar
- 1 tsp. or 2.46gm Cocoa Powder
- Drop of Red Colouring, optional

Method of Preparation:

1) To start with, combine coconut flour, sugar, salt, cocoa powder, almond flour, and baking powder in a large microwave-safe bowl until mixed well.

2) After that, combine milk with egg white in another bowl until mixed well.

3) Pour the milk mixture into the mug. Mix well until you get a smooth dough. Tip: Add colouring if using.

4) With a spoon, smoothen the surface of the dough so that it fills the bottom portion of the mug evenly.

5) Heat it on high heat for 1 minute or until cooked. If it seems raw, cook them at intervals of 30-seconds.

6) Allow it to cool for a few minutes before serving.

7) Serve and enjoy.

Tips:

- Instead of cocoa powder, you can use beet powder.

- You can add chocolate chips to it if desired.

- Instead of dairy milk, you can use any plant-based milk.

- To make the mug cake vegan, substitute an egg with a flax egg.

- Serve it with a topping of cream cheese frosting or dust it with powdered sugar.

Variation:

- You can also make it with regular all-purpose flour. For making with it, use three tablespoons of milk, ½ teaspoon of vinegar, two tablespoons of sugar, one teaspoon of cocoa powder, one and a half tablespoons of vegetables, a dash of salt, ¼ teaspoon of baking powder oil, and one teaspoon of cocoa powder along with one to two drops of food colouring if needed. Next, combine milk with vinegar in a small bowl. Stir all the dry ingredients in the mug, and then pour the milk-vinegar mixture into it. Give a good stir until everything comes together. Finally, heat it for 60 to 90 seconds or until cooked.

Nutritional Information per serving:

- **Calories**: 532Kcal
- **Carbohydrates**: 60g
- **Fat**: 30g
- **Proteins**: 11g

DESSERTS

35. Brownie in a Mug

The easiest chocolate dessert that you can make!

Preparation Time: 5 Minutes

Cooking Time: 1 to 2 Minutes

Servings: 1

Ideal Size of the Mug: 12oz.

Ingredients:

- ¼ tsp. or 1.5gm Vanilla Extract

- 2 tbsp. or 18gm Cocoa Powder, unsweetened

- 2 tbsp. or 28gm Chocolate Chips

- 3 tbsp. or 45ml Milk

- 3 tbsp. or 24gm All-Purpose Flour

- 2 ½ tbsp. or 27.8gm Vegetable Oil

- 3 tbsp. or 36gm Sugar, granulated
- Pinch of Salt

Method of Preparation:

1) Start by mixing flour, salt, sugar, cocoa powder, and salt in a short & wide microwave-safe bowl.

2) After that, stir in milk, vanilla extract, and oil to it.

3) Whisk the mix with a fork until everything comes together. Tip: Do not overmix, as it can harden the brownie.

4) Now, add ¾ of the chocolate chips to it while reserving ¼ of it for toppings.

5) Heat it for 1 minute on high heat. Tip: At this point, the brownie has risen and will look moist in certain areas. If it seems raw, cook in 10-second intervals until it is cooked to your desired consistency. Ensure the brownie doesn't get overcooked, as it will become very dry.

6) Allow it to cool for a few minutes before serving.

7) Serve and enjoy.

Tips:

- If preferred, you can top it with vanilla ice cream.
- Instead of white granulated sugar, you can use brown sugar.
- Semi-sweet chocolate chips would be the best choice for this brownie recipe.
- If it seems to have too much chocolate flavor, reduce the quantity of cocoa powder or add bicarbonate of soda.
- Instead of chocolate chips, you can use chopped chocolate.

Nutritional Information per serving:

- **Calories**: 874Kcal
- **Carbohydrates**: 100g
- **Fat**: 11g

- **Proteins:** 10g

36. Bread in a Mug

An easy bread recipe to make in the microwave that you can even toast later.

Preparation Time: 2 Minutes

Cooking Time: 1 to 2 Minutes

Servings: 1

Ideal Size of the Mug: 14oz.

Ingredients:

- 4 tbsp. or 28g All-Purpose Flour
- 2 tbsp. or 30ml Milk, whole

Method of Preparation:

1) Begin by placing the flour in a large microwave-safe bowl, and to this, pour the milk.

2) Mix well until you get a smooth dough. Tip: The dough should be wet and sticky. If the dough seems dry, add a tablespoon or more of milk.

3) With a spoon, smoothen the surface of the dough so that it fills the bottom portion of the mug evenly.

4) Heat it on high heat for 30 seconds or until cooked. If it seems raw, cook them in intervals until cooked.

5) Serve and enjoy.

Tips:

- Instead of milk, you can use unsweetened almond or cashew milk.
- For enhancing the flavor, you can use garlic powder or rosemary.
- For a richer taste, you can include eggs.

Nutritional Information per serving:

- **Calories**: 56Kcal

- **Carbohydrates**: 12g
- **Fat**: 1g
- **Proteins:** 2g

37. Rice- Krispie Treat

How about enjoying single-servings of crispy, crunchy & buttery rice krispies at night? What's more, you can make them in less than 5 minutes.

Preparation Time: 2 Minutes

Cooking Time: 1 Minute

Servings: 1

Ideal Size of the Mug: 16oz.

Ingredients:

- 9 Marshmallows, large
- ½ tbsp. or 7gm Butter, unsalted
- 1 cup or 25gm Rice Krispies Cereal

Method of Preparation:

1) Begin by placing the butter in a large microwave-safe bowl and heat it for 30 seconds on high heat.

2) Once the butter has melted, stir the marshmallows and butter well. Tip: The marshmallows can puff up, so do not overfill the cup.

3) Next, add half of the rice Krispies into it immediately and mix well. Then, add the remaining ones. Combine.

4) Serve and enjoy.

Tips:

- Instead of butter, you can use coconut oil.
- Instead of rice Krispies, you can use other cereals like cheerios, fruity pebbles, or Chex.
- To make it more delicious, add butterscotch chips or peanut butter.
- Dash of ground cinnamon is another excellent add-in.

Nutritional Information per serving:

- **Calories:** 561Kcal
- **Carbohydrates:** 127g
- **Fat:** 7g
- **Proteins:** 4g

38. Rice Pudding in a Mug

How about a creamy, lightly spiced rice pudding mug as your sweet treat? Fret not, for you can make this one in less than 10 minutes.

Preparation Time: 5 Minutes
Cooking Time: 2 to 3 Minutes
Servings: 1
Ideal Size of the Mug: 16oz.

Ingredients:

- 2 tbsp. or 24gm Sugar
- 2 tbsp. or 20gm Raisins
- ¼ cup or 60ml Milk, whole
- Dash of Salt
- 1 drop of Vanilla Extract
- 1 tbsp. or 15gm Heavy Cream
- ¾ cup or 155gm Rice, cooked
- ¼ tsp. or 0.7gm Cinnamon, grounded

Method of Preparation:

1) Begin by placing the sugar, heavy cream, salt, vanilla extract, ground cinnamon, and milk in a large microwave-safe bowl and whisk it well.

2) To this, stir in the rice and raisins.

3) Now, heat on high heat for 1 ½ to 2 minutes in 30-seconds intervals or until the mixture is thickened.

4) Set it aside for 5 minutes. Garnish with roasted almonds and raisins if desired.

5) Once cooled, place in the refrigerator to chill.

6) Serve and enjoy.

Tips:

- Arborio rice or sticky rice would be the preferred choice. But then, any long-grain rice would be suitable for this recipe.

- If you have leftover rice, this recipe would be an excellent way to use it.

- You can also top it with lemon zest or any citrus zest. Whipped cream also goes well as a topping for this pudding.

Variation:

- To make the pudding richer, add an egg if preferred. Whisk it well with the sugar, and then add the remaining ingredients. Heat at medium heat and cook for 6 minutes as too much heat may sometime cause the custard to separate.

Nutritional Information per serving:

- **Calories**: 382Kcal
- **Carbohydrates**: 72.1g
- **Fat**: 5.7g
- **Proteins**: 9.2g

39. Apple Crisp in Mug

With oatmeal crisp topping and caramel apples, this fall dessert made in the microwave can satisfy your craving in the best possible way.

Preparation Time: 5 Minutes
Cooking Time: 3 Minutes
Servings: 1
Ideal Size of the Mug: 14oz.

Ingredients:

- 1 Apple or 150gm, peeled & thinly sliced
- 1 tsp. or 3.3gm Flour
- ½ tbsp. or 7gm Butter, melted
- 1 tsp. or 4.17g Brown Sugar
- ¼ tsp. or 0.7gm Cinnamon, grounded

For the topping:

- 1 tbsp. or 12.5gm Brown Sugar
- 2 tbsp. or 14gm Butter, softened
- 1 tbsp. Pecan, finely chopped
- ¼ tsp. or 0.7gm Cinnamon, grounded
- 1 tbsp. or 10gm Flour
- 3 tbsp. or 30gm Old-Fashioned Oats

Method of Preparation:

1) First, combine all the ingredients needed to make the apple filling in a small bowl until mixed well.

2) After that, mix all the ingredients needed to make the crisp topping.

3) Now, layer half the apples in a microwave-safe bowl and top it with half of the crisp topping mixture.

4) Then, layer the remaining apples on top of the crisp mixture. Layer the remaining crisp above the apples.

5) Heat on high heat for 3 minutes. Allow it to cool for a few minutes. Stir the mixture halfway through the cooking time. Tip: Around the 2nd minute, the apples will start bubbling and will reduce in size.

6) Serve and enjoy.

Tips:

- If preferred, you can top it with vanilla ice cream.

- To reduce sweetness, you can lower the quantity of brown sugar used.

Nutritional Information per serving:

- **Calories**: 512Kcal
- **Carbohydrates**: 61g
- **Fat**: 30g
- **Proteins**: 4g

40. Bread Pudding in a Mug

Here comes a recipe for making warm and comforting cornbread easily and quickly in the microwave.

Preparation Time: 2 Minutes

Cooking Time: 3 Minutes

Servings: 1

Size of the mug: 12 oz.

Ingredients:

- ¼ tsp. or 1.5gm Vanilla Extract
- 2 Bread Sweet Rolls
- 1/3 or 80ml cup Milk
- 2 tbsp. or 28gm Chocolate Chips
- Dash of Cinnamon
- Pinch of Nutmeg
- 1 Egg or 40gm
- 2 tbsp. or 24gm Sugar

Method of Preparation:

1) First, slice the bread rolls into two and butter each side.

2) Slice each side into cubes.

3) After that, combine egg, vanilla, sugar, cinnamon, and milk in a small bowl.

4) Then, place the buttered bread cubes and chocolate chips in a greased large microwave-safe mug.

5) Stir in the egg mixture on top of the bread cubes.

6) With the help of a fork, pierce down the bread cubes into the egg mixture until it is completely covered.

7) Sprinkle nutmeg over it.

8) Finally, heat it for 60 seconds or until the egg is cooked and set. Cook for further 30 seconds. Tip: Cook for more time in 30-second intervals until cooked.

9) Allow it to cool for a few minutes before serving.

10) Serve and enjoy.

Tips:

- You can use any kind of bread to make this recipe.

- Instead of chocolate chips, you can use hazelnut spread, peanut butter, or Nutella.

- If preferred, you can top it with browned butter vanilla sauce. For this, you would require butter, vanilla, brown sugar, and milk. Melt the butter in a saucepan, and to this, add the brown sugar and milk. Cook for medium heat for 5 to 8 minutes or until thickened.

Nutritional Information per serving:

- **Calories**: 387Kcal
- **Carbohydrates**: 58g
- **Fat**: 14g
- **Proteins:** 11g

EXTRA RECIPES

41. Granola

This granola recipe can come in handy when you want a healthy and nutritious breakfast that can be made quickly and easily.

Preparation Time: 2 Minutes
Cooking Time: 3 Minutes
Servings: 1
Ideal Size of the Mug: 16oz.

Ingredients:

- 2 tbsp. or 10gm Nuts of your choice
- 2 tsp. or 9gm Coconut Oil
- 1 tbsp. or 10gm Raisins
- 1 tbsp. or 5.6gm Desiccated Coconut
- ¼ tsp. or 1.5 gm Vanilla Extract
- 5 tbsp. or 50gm Rolled Oats

- 2 tsp. or 14gm Honey
- Water, as needed

Method of Preparation:

1) To start with, combine coconut oil, honey, vanilla extract, and water in a large microwave mug until mixed well. Tip: Stir well, so it doesn't get stuck to the bottom of the mug.

2) Heat on high heat for 20 seconds.

3) After that, stir the oats, desiccated coconut, and nuts into the mixture. Tip: The oats and nuts should get properly coated with the liquid.

4) Continue cooking for another 1 ½ to 2 minutes. Stir halfway through the cooking time. At this point, the oats should start getting browned. If not, cook in 30-second increments while making sure to stir well.

5) Now, transfer the mixture to a plate and allow it to cool. Add the raisins. Tip: Do not add raisins at the beginning, as there is a chance for them to get browned & burnt.

6) Serve and enjoy.

Tips:

- You can add your choices of seeds, like chia seeds or flax seeds.
- Honey can be substituted with maple syrup or agave syrup.
- You can have the granola on its own or serve it with Greek yogurt or cashew yogurt.

Nutritional Information per serving:

- **Calories:** 350Kcal
- **Carbohydrates:** 40.5g
- **Fat:** 17.7g
- **Proteins:** 6.7g

42. Pumpkin Quinoa Porridge

Warm and comforting, this pumpkin quinoa fare can be quickly made in the microwave with just a few essential ingredients.

Preparation Time: 5 Minutes
Cooking Time: 3 Minutes
Servings: 1
Ideal Size of the Mug: 14oz.

Ingredients:

- 1/3 cup or 60gm Quinoa, cooked
- 1 tbsp. or 19.5gm Maple Syrup
- 1/3 cup or 75gm Pumpkin Puree
- ¼ tsp. or 0.45gm Pumpkin Pie Spice
- 2 Eggs or 80gm
- ¼ tsp. or 1.5gm Salt

Method of Preparation:

1) First, combine pumpkin, quinoa, pie spice, salt, and maple syrup in a large microwave-safe mug.

2) Heat on high heat for 3 minutes or until the middle portion is set and cooked.

3) Top it with nuts or seeds or dried fruits.

4) Serve and enjoy.

Tips:

- Instead of pumpkin puree, you can use mashed banana.

- If desired, you can add shredded coconut for more flavor.

- A dash of ground cinnamon is another excellent add-in for the fare.

- Instead of maple syrup, you can use brown sugar or honey.

- Top it with sliced fruits like apples and pears to make it more nutritious.

Nutritional Information per serving:

- **Calories**: 315Kcal

- **Carbohydrates**: 45g

- **Fat**: 7g

- **Proteins:** 8.5g

43. Cornbread in a Mug

Here comes a recipe for making warm and comforting cornbread easily and quickly in the microwave.

Preparation Time: 2 Minutes

Cooking Time: 1 to 2 Minutes

Servings: 1

Ideal Size of the Mug: 12oz.

Ingredients:

- ½ cup or 68gm All-Purpose Flour
- 2 tbsp. or 26.8gm Canola Oil
- ½ cup or 60gm Cornmeal
- 1 Egg or 40gm
- 3 tbsp. or 45ml of Milk
- 2 tbsp. or 24gm Sugar
- ¼ tsp. or 1.5gm Salt

Method of Preparation:

1) First, place all the ingredients in a greased large microwave-safe bowl.

2) Heat it on high heat for 2 to 3 minutes. Tip: Once two minutes have passed, remove the mug from the oven and insert a toothpick. If it comes clean, it is done.

3) Allow the cornbread to cool slightly before serving.

4) Serve and enjoy.

Tips:

- If desired, you can top it with honey butter. For this, combine 2 tablespoons of butter with one tablespoon of honey. Combine until smooth and top it over the bread.

- To make it spicier, you can add finely chopped jalapenos to it.

- Instead of canola oil, you can use melted butter.

- Serve it along with potato soup or pumpkin chili.

Nutritional Information per serving:

- **Calories**: 190Kcal
- **Carbohydrates**: 25g
- **Fat**: 3g
- **Proteins:** 9g

44. Hot & Sour Soup

With just 4 minutes, you can make this tasty yet healthy soup.

Preparation Time: 2 Minutes

Cooking Time: 4 to 5 Minutes

Servings: 1

Ideal Size of the Mug: 16oz.

Ingredients:

- 1 Scallion or 15gm, sliced thinly

- 1 cup or 250ml Chicken Stock, low-sodium

- Salt & Freshly Grounded Black Pepper

- ½ of 1 Egg (20gm), whisked

- 1 tbsp. or 16.6gm Soya Sauce, preferably low sodium

- 1 ½ tbsp. or 22ml Water

- ½ tbsp. or 7.2gm Rice Wine Vinegar

- 1 tbsp. or 7.5gm Cornstarch

- ¼ tsp. or 1gm Chili Oil
- 2 Cremini Mushrooms or 100gm
- ¼ cup or 30gm Tofu, firm

Method of Preparation:

1) To start with, combine water and cornstarch in a small bowl until mixed well. Keep it aside. Tip: The cornstarch should be completely dissolved in water.

2) Then, combine stock, rice vinegar, soya sauce, and chili oil in a large microwave-safe mug or bowl.

3) Check for seasoning and add more salt and pepper to it if needed.

4) Then, add mushrooms and tofu to it. Stir well.

5) Cook on high heat for 2 minutes. Stir again and continue cooking for another 1 minute or until the mushrooms are cooked.

6) Now, add the cornflour paste to it. Tip: Ensure that the slurry is not separated before adding since it will otherwise cause the cornstarch to clump together. Stir until the paste is completely dissolved into it.

7) Drizzle the whisked egg over the top and sprinkle black pepper powder over it. Whisk it with a fork a few times or until you see the eggs start to ribbon. Tip: The mixture should be hot enough such that the egg cooks partially in it.

8) Finally, cook for one minute or until it is thickened and the egg is cooked thoroughly.

9) Top it with scallions before serving.

10) Serve and enjoy.

Tips:

- Instead of cremini mushrooms, you can use shitake mushrooms. But it has a more robust flavor.

- For a spicier version, you can add more chili oil. Chili oil can be substituted with sriracha sauce.

- Whisk the egg well before adding it to the soup.

- For more flavor, you can use beef broth instead of chicken broth.

- Rice wine vinegar can be substituted with white vinegar though the flavor will be less.

Nutritional Information per serving:

- **Calories**: 184Kcal
- **Carbohydrates**: 16g
- **Fat**: 7g
- **Proteins:** 15g

45. Brown Rice Meal

This vegetarian microwave meal can come to your rescue when you want a meal without meat.

Preparation Time: 2 Minutes
Cooking Time: 7 Minutes
Servings: 1
Ideal Size of the Mug: 16oz.

Ingredients:

- 2 tbsp. or 18gm Cashews, chopped
- ½ cup or 125gm Instant Brown Rice
- 1 tbsp. or 18gm Teriyaki Sauce
- ¼ cup or 56gm Pineapple, finely diced
- 1/3 cup or 51gm Shelled Edamame, frozen
- 2/3 cup or 157ml of Water

Method of Preparation:

1) First, place rice and water in a large microwave-safe bowl.

2) After that, top it with edamame and cover it with a plastic wring. Poke holes in it with a fork.

3) Heat it on high heat for 5 to 6 minutes or until the rice is cooked and the water has been absorbed.

4) Take the mug out and allow it to cool for a minute or two.

5) Then, stir in the diced pineapple and teriyaki sauce.

6) Heat for 30 to 45 seconds or until the pineapple is warmed through.

7) Check for seasoning and add more if needed.

8) Top it with the chopped cashews.

9) Serve and enjoy.

Tips:

- To make a spicier version, add hot sauce like sriracha sauce.

- If desired, garnish it with green onions and mint leaves.

Nutritional Information per serving:

- **Calories**: 519Kcal
- **Carbohydrates**: 89.2g
- **Fat**: 12.2g
- **Proteins:** 14.4g

46. Mug Chili

Want a chili fare that you can make easily within 10 minutes and that too in the microwave? Then, here comes a high-protein one.

Preparation Time: 5 Minutes
Cooking Time: 5 Minutes
Servings: 1
Ideal Size of the Mug: 14oz.

Ingredients:

- ¾ cup or 150gm Crushed Tomatoes
- ¼ tsp. or 1.5gm Garlic Powder
- ¼ cup or 35gm Red Bell Pepper, chopped
- ½ tsp. or 1.5gm Cumin
- 1 tsp. or 2gm Chili Seasoning
- 2 tbsp. or 7.8gmCorn Kernels
- 2 tbsp. or 34gm Onion, chopped
- ¼ cup or 56gm Chili beans
- 2 oz. or 56gm Chicken, cooked & chopped

Method of Preparation:

1) First, place onion, water, and bell pepper in a large microwave mug.

2) Cover it with a plastic wring and pierce holes with a fork.

3) Heat for 90 seconds or until softened.

4) Now, add all the remaining ingredients to it and combine well.

5) Cover it with the plastic wring and cook for 2 minutes or until it becomes hot.

6) Serve and enjoy.

Tips:

- Top it with sour cream, green onion, and cubed avocado.

- You can also garnish it with cilantro leaves.

- To make it spicier, you can add tabasco sauce.

- For more flavor, you can try adding Worcestershire sauce.

- Instead of chili beans, you can use regular red kidney beans.

- To thicken the chili, you can add refried beans if desired.

- Salsa is another excellent add-in for chili.

Nutritional Information per serving:

- **Calories**: 254Kcal
- **Carbohydrates**: 32g
- **Fat**: 2.5g
- **Proteins:** 24.5g

47. Chilaquiles

A highly-satisfying Mexican fare that can be easily made in the microwave.

Preparation Time: 5 Minutes

Cooking Time: 5 Minutes

Servings: 1

Ideal Size of the Mug: 12oz.

Ingredients:

- 1 tbsp. Salsa
- 1 tbsp. or 15ml Milk
- 1 Egg or 40gm, beaten
- 5 Tortilla Chips
- Kosher Salt & Freshly Grounded Black Pepper
- 1 tbsp. or 7.6gm Cheddar Cheese, sharp & shredded

Method of Preparation:

1) Start by placing egg, milk, pepper, and salt in a greased large microwave-safe bowl. Whisk with a fork.

2) Then, stir the shredded cheese into the mix and combine well.

3) Next, add the chip pieces and salsa. Mix well.

4) Now, cook at high heat for 1 ½ minute or until cooked.

5) Serve and enjoy.

Tips:

- Top it with green onion and queso fresco.

- If desired, you can crush the tortilla chips and add them.

- If you wish to make it spicier, add hot sauce.

- Instead of sharp cheddar cheese, you can use Mexican blend cheese or Monterey Jack Cheese.

- Top it with red chili flakes for an extra kick.

Nutritional Information per serving:

- **Calories**: 300Kcal
- **Carbohydrates**: 34.5g
- **Fat**: 12.4g
- **Proteins**: 14.6g

48. Vegetable Soup

A simple soup that can be easily made in the microwave.

Preparation Time: 2 Minutes

Cooking Time: 4 to 5 Minutes

Servings: 1

Ideal Size of the Mug: 16oz.

Ingredients:

- 1 Egg or 40gm
- ½ of 1 or 35gm Carrot, finely chopped
- 1 tbsp. Bouillon
- 1 Celery Stalk or 40gm
- Water, as needed
- 1 Jalapeno Pepper or 15gm, finely chopped
- 1 tbsp. Onion, finely chopped

Method of Preparation:

1) Begin by placing carrots, jalapenos, celery, and bouillon in a large microwave-safe mug.

2) Next, add enough water to cover the vegetables fully. Tip: Ensure at least 1-inch of place is left on the top.

3) Then, cook for 2 to 3 minutes or until the veggies are cooked. Tip: Check frequently to make sure that the soup doesn't overboil.

4) Then, crack the egg and stir gently with a fork.

5) Finally, cook again for another 2 minutes or until the egg has begin to ribbon and is cooked.

6) Top it with scallions before serving.

7) Serve and enjoy.

Tips:

- You can add your choice of veggies to it, like mushrooms, etc.

- Cooked & finely shredded chicken and turkey are also excellent add-ins.

Nutritional Information per serving:

- **Calories**: 184Kcal
- **Carbohydrates**: 16g
- **Fat**: 7g
- **Proteins**: 15g

49. Pesto Mug Pasta

This vegetarian microwave meal can come to your rescue when you want a meal without meat.

Preparation Time: 5 Minutes
Cooking Time: 10 Minutes
Servings: 1
Ideal Size of the Mug: 16oz.

Ingredients:

- 2 tbsp. or 28gm Parmesan Cheese
- ½ cup or 50gm Pasta
- 1 cup or 240ml of Water
- ½ cup or 65gm Cooked Chicken, finely shredded
- Dash of Salt
- ½ cup or 15gm Spinach
- ½ cup or 114gm Cherry Tomatoes, halved
- Red Pepper Flakes, as needed
- 1 ½ tbsp. or 21gm Pesto

Method of Preparation:

1) To begin with, place the pasta and 2/3rd cup of water in a large microwave-safe mug. Add salt and stir well.

2) After that, keep a plate under the mug and heat it in the microwave for 5 minutes. Turn it once halfway during the cooking time. Stir and cook for the remaining minutes.

3) Once the time is up, stir and add the remaining water to it and cook for 2 to 3 minutes or until the pasta is cooked.

4) Then, add the pesto to the cooked pasta. Mix until the pesto coats the pasta well.

5) Next, stir in the spinach, tomatoes, and chicken to it.

6) Continue cooking for another 30 to 60 seconds or until the spinach has wilted and the tomatoes have broken down.

7) Finally, add the cheese and red pepper flakes immediately while it is warm.

8) Serve and enjoy.

Tips:

- You can choose smaller pasta for this recipe.

- To make it vegetarian, you can swap the chicken with beans.

- Instead of parmesan cheese, you can select your favorite cheese for it.

Nutritional Information per serving:

- **Calories**: 370Kcal

- **Carbohydrates**: 28g

- **Fat**: 14g

- **Proteins**: 31g

50. Chow Mein in a Mug

This mug version of chow-mein is easy to make while being lip-smacking.

Preparation Time: 5 Minutes

Cooking Time: 2 Minutes

Servings: 1

Ideal Size of the Mug: 16oz.

Ingredients:

- 2 tbsp. or 20gm Shredded Carrot
- ½ cup or 37.5gm of Noodles
- 1 tbsp. or 13.3gm Olive Oil
- 1 tsp. or 2gm Ginger, grated
- ½ cup or 100ml Vegetable Broth
- Salt & Pepper, to taste
- 2 tbsp. Water
- 1 Spring Onion, chopped

- 2 tsp. or 10gm Soy Sauce
- ½ tsp. Dried Garlic
- ½ of 1 or 70gm Green Bell Pepper, finely diced

Method of Preparation:

1) First, place noodles, salt, oil, and vegetable broth in a large microwave-safe bowl and stir.

2) Cook the noodles for 3 minutes or until the noodles are cooked. Stir the mixture once during the cooking time.

3) Now, add all the remaining ingredients to it and give a good stir until everything comes together.

4) Cook for further 2 minutes on high heat. Mix well.

5) Serve and enjoy.

Tips:

- You can use dried chow-mein noodles for this recipe.
- If you wish to make the sauce for the noodles thicker, you can add cornstarch.
- Bean sprouts, mushrooms, and cabbage are excellent veggies to add to this recipe.
- You can use sesame oil instead of olive oil.

Nutritional Information per serving:

- **Calories**: 331Kcal
- **Carbohydrates**: 31g
- **Fat**: 22g
- **Proteins:** 4g

THANK YOU FOR FINISHING THE BOOK!

We would like to thank you very much for supporting us and reading through to the end. We know you could have picked any number of books to read, but you picked this book and for that, we are extremely grateful.

We hope you enjoyed your reading experience. If so, it would be really nice if you could share this book with your friends and family by posting it on Facebook and Twitter.

Lion Weber Publishing stands for the highest reading quality and we will always endeavor to provide you with high-quality books.

Would you mind leaving us a review before you go? Because it will mean a lot to us and support us in creating high-quality guidelines for you in the future.

Please help us reach more readers by taking 30 seconds to write just a few words on Amazon now.

Warmly,
The Lion Weber Publishing Team

Made in United States
North Haven, CT
15 November 2022

26792156R00068